"BEHOLD THE LAMB!"

Nihil Obstat.
J. N. STRASSMAIER, S.J.
CENSOR DEPUTATUS.

Imprimatur.
EDM. CAN. SURMONT,
VICARIUS GENERALIS.

WESTMONASTERII,
Die 26 Septembris, 1912.

First published by Burn & Oates, 1912
Copyright 2007 Catholic Authors Press

ISBN: 978-0-9782985-4-8

Catholic Authors Press

Hartford, Connecticut

www.CatholicAuthors.org

"SUFFER LITTLE CHILDREN TO COME UNTO ME."

Frontispiece.

"BEHOLD THE LAMB!"

A BOOK FOR LITTLE FOLKS ABOUT THE HOLY MASS

BY

MARIE St. S. ELLERKER
TERTIARY, O S.D.

WITH PREFACE BY
VERY REV. VINCENT McNABB, O.P.

Catholic Authors Press
www.CatholicAuthors.com

Contents

CONTENTS

	PAGE
PREFACE BY VERY REV. VINCENT McNABB, O.P., S.T.B.	ix
I. WHAT IT IS	11
II. DEBTS	17
III. IN YOUR NAME AND IN YOUR PLACE	22
IV. WORDS	26
V. GOD'S LESSONS: (1) THE LAMB	30
VI. „ „ (2) THE SCAPEGOAT	34
VII. „ „ (3) PRIEST AND KING	39
VIII. „ „ (4) TOLD BEFOREHAND	43
IX. A BEAUTIFUL TITLE	48
X. MY CRUCIFIX	54
XI. "IN MEMORY OF ME"	59
XII. IN THE SCHOOL OF OUR BLESSED LORD	63
XIII. A MARRIAGE FEAST	68
XIV. BEHIND THE VEILS	73

Contents

		PAGE
XV. In a Desert	- - -	78
XVI. A Promise	- - -	83
XVII. A Man with a Pitcher	-	89
XVIII. The Work of a Slave	-	95
XIX. Corpus Christi	- -	101

ILLUSTRATIONS

	TO FACE PAGE
"Suffer Little Children to come unto Me"	*Frontispiece*
"O Salutaris Hostia"	22
"Behold the Lamb of God!"	32
"You are bought with a Great Price"	54
The Mystery of Faith	101

Preface

PREFACE

THIS book is written, first of all, for Jesus in the Blessed Sacrament.

If Jesus is a King, and exiled amongst us for love of us, it is only fair that we should give Him some noble gift. We shall think our best unworthy of Him; but He will be as glad of it as we are glad of the sea or of the sun.

This land, where once the Church of God was the Church of the people, is full of splendid gifts to the King who has become like a little lamb upon our hillsides. Few lands have so many or so fair churches, now many of them, alas! in ruin. We are building new churches for Him, and furnishing them with beautiful vessels of silver and gold made by the skilled hands of love. Above all, we are pleasing Him most by filling His

Preface

dwelling-place with those who love to be with Him and to sit down at His board.

This book has been made, and is given, as a gift to Him. If no one ever read it, if it never kindled a new thought or touched any heart, it would still be His.

Yet, as it is His, and He and all He has are ours, this book is meant for us. It has been written for little children—of all ages. The most childlike children are often those who are quite old. The Child whom we worship by this book is the Eternal Son.

The Blessed Sacrament is that Kingdom of Heaven whose golden streets no one can tread unless he has the pure white feet and purer heart of a little child.

May He to whom first of all this book is given bless its pages for those to whom it and He are alike given!

VINCENT McNABB, O.P.

"BEHOLD THE LAMB!"

I

WHAT IT IS

This is a little book for little people about a very great present from "Holy God."

The Blessed Sacrament is God's most wonderful gift to you and me.

Have you ever read "A Wonder Book for Girls and Boys," by Nathaniel Hawthorne? When I first heard the title, I wanted it at once. Doing lessons, going for walks, and being put to bed, with meals in between, though quite nice, are so ordinary; but the very word "wonder" means something quite

"Behold the Lamb!"

different from such commonplace, every-day things.

Once, long after I had read Hawthorne's delightful stories, a Missal or Mass Book was put into my hands for the very first time, and the thought that flashed instantly through my mind was, "This is Almighty God's Wonder Book."

We are obliged to go to Mass every Sunday and holiday of obligation if we are able, otherwise we should commit a mortal sin; but some, even amongst those who never miss, wish that they were not obliged to go. This is because they do not know enough of the *wonders* of Holy Mass, and so to them it seems dull—a commonplace thing.

I should like to tell you enough about these wonders to make you realize that nothing in the whole world

What it is

can be compared with the Holy Mass; to make you feel it to be the most wonderfully interesting thing in your lives, and to make you love it so much that your greatest and truest joy will be to hear it, not only when you are obliged, but as often as ever God gives you the opportunity.

You must often have heard big people use the phrase, "The Holy Sacrifice of the Mass"; perhaps the priest said it when he was giving out the notices on Sunday. Now, if anyone stopped you and asked suddenly, "What do you think *sacrifice* means?" could you explain to them? It is not really difficult to understand, but there are a good many things which we must not forget. We will put them out on separate lines.

Sacrifice is—

1. Something which is offered to

"Behold the Lamb!"

Holy God, and never to anyone else, not even our Blessed Lady.

2. The thing which is offered must be something we can see, hear, taste, touch, or smell.

3. It must be offered by a person chosen by God.

4. This person must destroy or completely change the thing.

5. He must do this to show that God is the great Master of all things, even of life and death.

The thing which is offered is called a victim.

The person who offers it is called a priest.

The idea that we ought to offer sacrifice to God seems to be planted deep down in the hearts of all people. When brave men have gone long, dangerous journeys to find out about

What it is

lands in which strange and sometimes savage people live, they have nearly always something to tell us of the way in which sacrifice is offered to the gods of these peoples.

And when we read history, whether it be from the Holy Bible, about Cain and Abel, or about our own country in far-off times, we find sacrifices were offered. Indeed, I remember that my first acquaintance with history was a blood-curdling tale of sacrifice, told graphically and with much detail by a brother, which kept me lying awake trembling, and then sent me horrid dreams.

I think, perhaps, you will like to end each little talk with a story.

Story.—Have you ever heard a person say, " So-and-so is too young to go to

"Behold the Lamb!"

Mass"? Such people are not at all like Blessed Joan of Aza, a noble Spanish lady. She asked God for a child, and He gave her a baby whom we know as St. Dominic.

Blessed Joan was accustomed to go to Mass every day, and every day she took with her her dear little baby. Possibly the very first thing he remembers is an altar, a vested priest, and, held high in consecrated hands, the pure white Host, the Body of Christ.

II
DEBTS

Do you feel rather afraid of the word *ought*? I always do.

You know that you *ought* to obey your mother, and she has a *right* to your obedience; you *ought* to be attentive in class, because your teacher has a *right* to your attention.

These things you ought to do are your *duties* and other people's *rights*. Of course you have rights, too, but I hope they will never, all your life, seem as important or as interesting to you as your duties. People who are never interested in anything but their *rights* are never very noble characters.

"Behold the Lamb!"

Let us talk for a few minutes about *God's rights* and *our duties*.

God made us. He gave us a body and a soul. Without Him we never should have lived at all, and we should not continue to live a minute. We depend entirely on this great, good God who is our Creator. Because He has made us He has the *right* to everything we have and everything we are; He has a right to the life He has given us. On our side it is our *duty* to own this, and this acknowledgement that we depend entirely upon God is one of the things we mean by adoration. We owe God a great debt of adoration as our Creator, and He would have the right to require us to pay this debt by giving back to Him in sacrifice this life He has given us.

Besides life, God has given us more

Debts

other things than we can number—faith, hope, love, the Sacraments, talents, parents, home, pleasures. For all, God has a *right* to our deepest gratitude, and it is our *duty* to thank Him. We owe God a second great debt of thanks, and He has the right to ask us to pay this debt by giving back to Him in sacrifice the dearest of our possessions—life.

Try, some time, to see how many things you can count that God has given to you for your body or for your soul.

When we sinned for the first time God might have punished us with death, and how many, many times we have sinned since then! Each time we deserved to die. What a debt of punishment for sin we owe to God! Not even by shedding our blood could we really make up for one of those sins,

"Behold the Lamb!"

but, at least, God would have the right to ask us to make up, as far as we are able, for offending Him, by offering to Him the sacrifice of our life.

Lastly, from God's loving kindness comes all we need. His goodness gives us heaven, and the means of reaching heaven. Only God can give us what we need, and it is our *duty* to beg Him earnestly to do so. In order to obtain life everlasting, God might have asked from us the sacrifice of the life we have here.

What tremendous debts we have; and we are so poor!

Story.—The Holy Mass can be offered only over the relics of a martyr. The Body of Christ is given to us only over a body which has been given to Him. During the persecution under the

Debts

Emperor Valerian, a number of the sacred ministers had been cast into prison, and were awaiting martyrdom. They wished to be strengthened for their sufferings by the Bread of Life, but alas! in their prison there was no altar stone. The Church is our mother, and for the dying she can sweep aside all rules. You would never guess in what a beautiful way they managed. The priests offered up the sacrifice of the Body and Blood of Jesus Christ upon the open hands of the deacons, who were soon to be the victims, instead of the altar.

III

IN YOUR NAME AND IN YOUR PLACE

The debts of which we spoke in the last chapter are paid to God by offering Him sacrifice. Yet He is so wonderfully good and pitiful that He has not commanded our own lives to be sacrificed to Him, but allows us to offer something else in our place.

In the far-off times it was sometimes a little lamb, or perhaps a dove. But even very little children know that since the day when our dear Lord died for us, we have another most wonderful sacrifice. Our dear Lord Himself is offered up in our name and in our place.

"O SALUTARIS HOSTIA."

To face p. 22.

In Your Name and in Your Place

When you go to Holy Mass you can say to yourself very slowly: "On the altar, Jesus, our dear Lord, is offering Himself instead of me, to pay my debt of adoration to God." Join yourself with Him in offering up this wonderful sacrifice.

In your name and in your place Jesus is offering Himself as a sacrifice of thanksgiving for all the things that God has given to you. He is paying your debt of gratitude. How glad you ought to feel that God is being thanked so well!

In your name and in your place Jesus is offering Himself at Holy Mass to beg God to forgive you your sins and the punishment you have deserved for them. This is one reason why you should never be afraid to go to confession, because Jesus in the Holy Mass has offered Himself in sacrifice for your sins

"Behold the Lamb!"

in order that you may be forgiven freely.

In your name and in your place Jesus is offering Himself in sacrifice, to implore God to give you everything you ask in His Name. Whenever you want God to grant you any grace or favour, go to Holy Mass and offer our dear Lord sacrificed there to obtain for you all that you need for seul and body. It is because Jesus is the Victim instead of us that we give Him one of the most beautiful of all the names by which He is called in the Blessed Sacrament—the Sacred *Host*. Host comes from a Latin word meaning a victim. He is our Victim. I should like you to love that name of His very much indeed.

Story.— A great King of France, Louis IX., was once praying in the

In Your Name and in Your Place

church, when someone ran to tell him to come quickly to an altar where the priest had just elevated the Sacred Host, and in it all could see our Lord as a little child! The King refused to go, saying he knew quite well that Jesus was in the Blessed Sacrament, because He had said so Himself, and he therefore had no need to see. He was perhaps thinking of the words of Jesus Christ: "Blessed are those who have not seen and have believed."

IV
WORDS

It is always trying, when we are reading about something, to have the same words coming over and over again, and to feel that we do not know quite what they mean.

Whenever we are reading or hearing about sacrifice, there are some words which are sure to be repeated again and again. We might take a few now, and try to get their meaning quite clear.

Offering.—This word is used for the thing or things which are given for the priest to offer to God. In old Catholic times the people offered the bread and wine for the Holy Sacrifice.

Words

Oblation.—This is the *act* of offering the bread and wine to God. The oblation must be made by a priest.

Offertory.—The name given to that part of Mass at which the priest makes the oblation. It is one of the three principal parts of Mass, and if you were not present during it you would not have heard Mass.

Immolation is a word which means the putting to death or destruction of the Victim. It is the chief act in all sacrifice; there could not be any sacrifice without it. We are going to have quite a separate talk later about the immolation of our dear Lord in the Holy Mass; I say that in case you feel just ready to get perplexed.

Communion.—This is the act by which we unite ourselves to the sacrifice by eating the flesh of the Victim. This is

"Behold the Lamb!"

the third principal part of Mass, at which all must be present, though all are not bound to communicate. The priest, however, must receive the Body and Blood of Jesus Christ in order to complete the sacrifice.

Instead of saying, as we did in another talk, that our Blessed Lord offers Himself in the Holy Mass—(1) To adore God in our name and in our place; (2) to thank Him for all He has done for us; (3) to obtain forgiveness for us; (4) to beg for all the graces we need, this is sometimes put in another way, as "The Four Ends of Holy Mass," and they are named as—

1. Adoration.
2. Thanksgiving.
3. Propitiation.
4. Supplication or Petition.

These are longer words, but they

Words

mean the same things, so you need not be afraid of them.

Story. — St. Wenceslaus, Duke of Bohemia, had the greatest possible devotion to the Blessed Sacrament, and loved to prepare with his own hands the altars and everything needed for Holy Mass. He himself made the altar breads, which were to be changed into the Body of Christ. A cornfield was set aside for this purpose, which the Duke tilled. He it was who sowed the seed, reaped the golden grain, and, after grinding it into the finest flour, would prepare the altar breads and humbly present them to the priest at Mass.

V
GOD'S LESSONS
1. The Lamb

You have known, dear children, what it was to come to some lesson and to feel that no matter how many times you read it, or how long you tried, never, never would you be able to understand or remember it. Then someone, perhaps a big brother, came along, and, seeing the trouble, took the book, called you "little duffer" in a way that did not hurt a bit, and showed you how the new lesson was very like something you had done before, how the old lesson led up to this one; and in a few minutes everything was quite clear.

God's Lessons

Now, before God gave His beloved Son to die on the Cross and to be our sacrifice in Holy Mass, He gave the world a great many lessons to lead up to it, lessons which had some likeness to the great Sacrifice to come. These likenesses are what are meant when you hear people talk about *types* of our Blessed Lord or of His Sacrifice. There were a number of them, but we are only going to talk of three.

Do you remember in your Old Testament history the story of the Ten Plagues of Egypt? In the last, God was going to send His Angel of Death into every house to slay the eldest child there. He wished, however, to spare His own people, the Jews, and this is what He bade them do. Each family was to take a little lamb, perfect and without spot. In the evening it was to be killed, and

"Behold the Lamb!"

its blood sprinkled on the door posts of all the houses in which God's people dwelt, and the flesh was to be eaten, with many ceremonies. During the night the Angel of Death went through the land of Egypt, but he passed over the houses on whose doors he saw the blood of the lamb which had been sacrificed, and no child died there.

Can you not see in how many ways this bore a kind of likeness to the spotless Lamb of God, whose Blood was shed and sprinkled upon our souls to preserve us from everlasting death?

Five times during Holy Mass the priest calls our Lord by this beautiful title; once in the *Gloria;* three times at the *Agnus Dei,* which is the Latin for "Lamb of God"; and once, when holding in his hand the Sacred Host which he is going to give in Holy

"BEHOLD THE LAMB OF GOD!"

To face p. 32.

God's Lessons

Communion, he says, "Behold the Lamb of God; behold Him who taketh away the sins of the world."

Instead of a story I think you will like these beautiful lines, which were written by Christina Rossetti:

> "A lamb is innocent and mild,
>   And merry on the soft green sod;
> And Jesus Christ, the Undefiled,
>   Is the Lamb of God.
> Only spotless, He
>   Upon His Mother's knee;
> White and ruddy, soon to be
>   Sacrificed for you and me."

VI

GOD'S LESSONS (*continued*)

2. The Scapegoat

DID you ever hear it said of some child always in disgrace, " He is the scapegoat!" meaning that he was often blamed for things done by others? Perhaps you did not know that the scapegoat was one of the Jewish sacrifices.

Two goats were brought to the priest, who drew lots to see which one should be killed and which should be the *scapegoat*. The one on whom the lot did *not* fall was immolated—that is, slain— as an offering for sin. Then the priest took the living goat and offered it to

God's Lessons

God with many prayers, and, putting both hands upon its head, the priest confessed the sins of the people, putting them, as it were, upon the goat. When he had finished he drove it out far into the wilderness, and it was seen no more.

If during your walk you had been accustomed to pass someone each day, and then a day came when you missed him from the accustomed place, and as day succeeded day, and the weeks went by, still the person did not appear, at last you would probably say, "I wonder if that man we used to see *is* dead;" because to be seen no more by our fellow-creatures is one of the effects of death.

Now the little goat did not really die, but it seemed to suffer the effects of death; it seemed as if it were dead; it was seen no more. This is sometimes

"Behold the Lamb!"

spoken of as *mystical death*; real death has not taken place, but there is an appearance of death.

This sacrifice was like our Lord on the Cross, and like the Holy Mass; like our Lord on the Cross because He, too, bore the sins of the people. God laid upon Him the sins of all. The prophet Isaias, speaking of Him, says: " He was wounded for our iniquities, He was bruised for our sins; the chastisement of our peace was upon Him, and by His bruises we are healed."

It is like our Lord in the Holy Mass, because there Jesus is not really slain, as He was on Calvary, but there is the appearance of death. His precious Blood seems to be separated from His Body, as when a person has died by violence.

Perhaps, if you ever happen to be

God's Lessons

blamed for something you have not done, instead of getting angry, you could think of our Blessed Lord bearing our sins, and say nothing, but just offer it, that you may be made a little more like Him.

Story.—I think you have heard of the holy nun who is most often called "The Little Flower of Jesus." It is very consoling to find that even holy people do not always find it easy to be good. She tells us a little story about herself when she was fifteen, and had just entered the convent. "I did my best," she writes, " not to make excuses. My first victory, though slight, cost me a good deal. A jar, left near a window, got broken. Our novice-mistress was displeased, and, supposing that it had been my fault, told me to be less dis-

"Behold the Lamb!"

orderly, and to take more care another time. I silently kissed the ground; but such a little act was great to me, because I had but little virtue, and I had to cheer myself with the thought that all would be known at the last day."

VII
GOD'S LESSONS (*continued*)

3. Priest and King

Long, long before our Blessed Lord came, God chose a holy man named Abraham, and told him to leave his own country to go to one which He would show him. God was going to do great things with Abraham, to make him the father of a mighty nation. You remember noticing in your New Testament that the Jews spoke of " our Father Abraham." From him our Lord Himself was to be descended.

Abraham is remarkable amongst the heroes of the Bible for his obedience, so when God told him to leave his own

" Behold the Lamb!"

country, he did so. Amongst those who went with him was his nephew, Lot.

Lot had a number of adventures; in one he was taken prisoner by the victors in a fight of " four kings against five." One prisoner escaped, and told Abraham of this misfortune; he at once set out with his friends and servants—" three hundred and eighteen, well appointed "— to rescue his nephew. He rushed upon the enemy at night, and won a complete victory, taking from them not only their prisoners, but a great deal of treasure.

On his way back we read that he was met by a mysterious person of whom we have heard nothing before. He is Melchisedech, King of Salem, priest of the most high God. We know nothing of his parents, of his house, or his life. He came and offered

God's Lessons

a sacrifice of thanksgiving to God for Abraham's victory.

If you have not heard the story before, you will never guess what his sacrifice was. We are told that he came " bringing forth bread and wine " —bread and wine to be offered in thanksgiving. The word " Eucharist " means thanksgiving.

Do you not feel at once what a beautiful type this is of the Holy Mass ? Of course, as you think and think, you see that, beautiful as it is, it is only like a beautiful shadow of which the Holy Mass is the reality. How good God has been to put us into the world since our dear Lord came to hide Himself under the appearances of bread and wine ! Think, dear little ones, what it would be like if, instead of your own beloved mother, you only had her shadow, or

"Behold the Lamb!"

a very poor photograph of her! That will give you some little idea of the difference.

Story.—A very beautiful story is told of the Emperor St. Henry. He was remarkable for his devotion to the Blessed Sacrament and his love of purity. When he arrived in any town it was his custom to spend the first night in a church, watching before the altar. As he was thus praying in the Church of St. Mary Major on the night of his arrival in Rome, he had a wonderful dream. He tells us that he "saw the Sovereign and Eternal Priest, Christ Jesus, enter to say Mass; with Him came St. Lawrence and St. Vincent, who assisted as deacon and sub-deacon."

VIII

GOD'S LESSONS (*continued*)

4. TOLD BEFOREHAND

I AM sure that by this time you are thinking that after so many lessons the Jews ought to have recognized our Blessed Lord's sacrifice quite easily. But God was not satisfied with giving them *types*. He even told them beforehand very many things about Jesus Christ, so that there might be no mistake when He came—about His mother, the place in which He should be born, the kind of life He should live, how He should die, and even about the Resurrection and Ascension. You can hardly believe it, but it is quite true.

" Behold the Lamb !"

If you were sent to meet someone at the station, and had been given all sorts of signs by which you could know them, and then, though they stood near, and even spoke to you, you arrived home without them, you would, at least, be thought very careless and inattentive, would you not?

Now the Jews were actually told by God Himself that the Redeemer they were expecting would have a holy Virgin Mother; that He would be born at Bethlehem; His star would be seen in the east, and kings would come from afar to offer Him gifts; that He would seek refuge in Egypt; that He would preach the Gospel to the poor, heal the sick, cleanse the lepers, raise the dead; that in the end He would be taken by His enemies, scourged, spat upon, and die, His sacred hands and feet nailed to

God's Lessons

the Cross, and His heart pierced by the lance; that He would not remain in the tomb, but rise again and ascend triumphantly to heaven.

You think I am telling you the life of Jesus Christ from the Gospels, but really I got all that from the Old Testament; it was told to the Jews hundreds of years before any of it happened at all.

This telling beforehand of something which is going to happen is called *Prophecy*, and it was one of God's most wonderful ways of teaching the people. We may be sure that if God told them so much in this way, He will have said something about the Holy Mass.

In a book of the Bible called Malachias there are these words: " From the rising of the sun to the going down, My Name is great amongst the Gentiles, and in every place there is sacrifice, and there is

"Behold the Lamb!"

offered to My Name a clean oblation, for My Name is great amongst the Gentiles, saith the Lord of hosts."

This prophecy is coming true every day, for somewhere on the surface of our earth, in our own country or some other, the Holy Mass is being offered up every hour of the day and night. Some people make a habit of offering to God as soon as they awake each morning all the Masses which will be said all over the world during the next twenty-four hours. During the day it is very beautiful and very consoling to think of the Masses being said at that moment, and to join ourselves to Jesus in the Sacred Host, especially when we are in pain or trouble.

Story.—St. Leonard of Port Maurice had a great devotion to the practice of

God's Lessons

which we have just spoken—he constantly offered to God all the Masses which were being said all over the world. He said his own Mass with the most wonderful devotion, always preparing for it by going to confession. Each day he heard as many as his duties permitted, and once, when someone remonstrated with him for this as a waste of time, he replied, "One Mass is worth more than all the treasure in the world."

IX
A BEAUTIFUL TITLE

Our dear Lord has many, many beautiful titles. Only last week I read of one in this line of poetry, which I feel sure you will like very much:

"Pearl of Great Price, within the monstrance set."

We have already spoken of two names by which we know Him in Holy Mass— "Lamb of God" and our "Host"—but if there is a victim to be offered we must have a priest, and it is of our Lord as our great Priest we are going to speak next.

I do not know how you picture our

A Beautiful Title

Blessed Lord to yourself when you are thinking about Him. Some imagine Him almost invariably as a Child in the arms of His Mother; others, crowned with thorns, as He was during His Passion. I always think of Him as a Priest holding the bread to be changed into His Body, or with His Hand raised to absolve and bless me.

In every Mass Jesus Christ Himself is the Chief Priest; through His ministers He says each Mass, consecrates each time the bread and wine. When you go to confession it is the wounded Hand of Jesus Christ, our High Priest, which is raised to loose you from your sins. When you receive the blessing of a priest, it is Jesus who blesses you through the priest.

In the Epistle to the Hebrews (one of the books of the New Testament),

" Behold the Lamb !"

the writer of the letter has put the most beautiful things about our dear Lord as our " High Priest." I think he must have had a great love for Him under that title. Shall I copy out two passages for you? In Chapter V. we have drawn for us the office of a human priest in these words:

" For every high priest taken from among men, is ordained for men in the things that appertain to God, that he may offer up gifts and sacrifices for sins: Who can have compassion on them that are ignorant and that err: because he himself also is compassed with infirmity: And therefore he ought, as for the people, so also for himself, to offer for sins. Neither doth any man take the honour to himself, but he that is called by God, as Aaron was."

Then follows a wonderful and very

A Beautiful Title

mysterious account of Christ as our High Priest. The writer himself finds it hard to make such high things quite clear to the ordinary mind, and says so quite simply. But we often feel something is very beautiful before we are able to understand it, and so I think you will like these verses.

"'Thou art My Son, this day have I begotten Thee.' As He (God) says also in another place: 'Thou art a priest for ever, according to the order of Melchisedech.' Who (our Lord) in the days of His flesh, with a strong cry and tears, offering up prayers and supplications to Him that was able to save Him from death, was heard for His reverence. And whereas, indeed, He was the Son of God, He learned obedience by the things which He suffered. And, being consummated, He became,

"Behold the Lamb!"

to all that obey Him, the cause of eternal salvation. Called by God a High Priest according to the order of Melchisedech. Of whom we have much to say, and hard to be intelligibly uttered."

St. Thomas Aquinas, the patron of all Catholic school-children, has written about this very Epistle to the Hebrews, and in one place says just what we have put above. He tells us it is Christ Himself who blesses by the hands of the priest. So when you see a priest at the altar, or kneel for one to absolve or bless you, think of our dear Lord, the invisible High Priest, present beside or within him. I like to think of the priest as a living monstrance through which I see the Son of God—"the Priest for ever according to the order of Melchisedech."

A Beautiful Title

You will think about all this in your own way, but in the end you will understand why we should show such great love, reverence, and respect for God's ministers.

Story.—St. Francis of Assisi used to say that if he were to meet a priest and an angel in the road, he would immediately kiss the priest's hand, and say to the angel: "Wait for me, dear angel, for this hand has touched the Word of Life."

When St. Jane Frances de Chantal was a tiny child, she had such a wonderful reverence for the sacred character of a priest that if she saw one she would run out and kiss the ground over which he had passed.

X

MY CRUCIFIX

THE Church tells us that Holy Mass is the memorial, the continuation, the application of the sacrifice of the Cross. It is not another sacrifice, but the same as our dear Lord offered on Calvary. So, in order to understand Mass, it seems as if we ought to spend a little time in trying to understand the Cross.

Take your crucifix in your hands, and let us see what we can find out about our Lord's sacrifice; it is full of the wonders of love.

Who is the Victim? It is Jesus Christ Himself as man. It is His own sacred Body which is immolated, not

"YOU ARE BOUGHT WITH A GREAT PRICE."

My Crucifix

the body of a little bird or lamb. In order to understand what it meant to our dear Lord to be the victim, look very carefully and lovingly at your crucifix. Touch the sacred Figure reverently with your little finger. First, the sacred Head, crowned with thorns; think of the worst pain you ever had in your head, and try to understand what just that one pain must have been. His Body was made like ours; it was exquisitely sensitive to pain, and sometimes to compare with His some little pain we have felt ourselves helps us to understand how much He must have loved us.

Go, then, to the wounded shoulders of Christ, all bleeding from the cruel whips; to the tender, loving Hands and Feet, pierced with the great nails—and we cry out if a pin pricks us! Jesus

"Behold the Lamb!"

accepted all that in accepting to stand in our place and be our Victim.

Who is the priest chosen by God to offer such a holy Victim? We feel certain at once that it is not a cruel soldier; God never commissioned anyone to commit the awful crime of killing his Saviour. It was Jesus Christ Himself who was Priest as well as Victim. He offered up His life for us by His own will. St. Augustine has said very beautifully that our Lord was the Victim in His Flesh and the Priest in His Soul.

To whom did this great High Priest offer up the sacrifice of His most holy Body? To the Blessed Trinity—three Persons in one God; to the Father and the Holy Ghost, and—a thought which has always seemed to me most wonderful—to Himself—God the Son.

My Crucifix

Why is He offering Himself thus? In sacrifice for our sins, to purchase eternal life for you and for me because He loves us.

For a sacrifice we need not only priest and victim, but also an altar, and our dear Lord had the terrible altar of the Cross.

Story.—A young girl, coming from a wealthy home, where she had been much petted, wished to become a nun. The Superior gave her a graphic picture of all the hard things she would find in the convent, and thought the young girl seemed to waver, but after a moment's pause, she asked: "Are there any crucifixes in the convent? Shall I find a crucifix in that narrow cell, with the hard bed of which you spoke? in that refectory, where the food is so coarse

"Behold the Lamb!"

and unpalatable? in that chapter, where such hard penance is done?"

"Oh yes," answered the nun, "there are crucifixes everywhere."

"Then I hope," the girl replied, "that I shall not find anything too difficult, since I shall have a crucifix with me wherever I am, and whatever I have to suffer."

XI

"IN MEMORY OF ME"

A VERY small boy was once confiding to me why he was in disgrace with his governess: "She gives such hard lessons, and the *explains* are harder."

There are some things we must try to understand about Holy Mass, but which, like the little boy, I think explanations sometimes make harder. I will put them down, and not explain at all.

The Church teaches us that the Mass is the same Sacrifice as that of the Cross.

In Holy Mass the Victim is the same —Jesus Christ, our Lord.

"Behold the Lamb!"

The Priest is the same; again it is our dear Lord.

The Sacrifice is offered to God for all; for the living and the dead.

On the Cross our Blessed Lord paid the price of all the graces we have received, or ever shall receive, from God.

At Holy Mass God gives to us, as we need them, all the benefits for which the Precious Blood of Jesus shed on Calvary was the price paid.

On the Cross our dear Lord really and truly died; His Precious Blood was all separated from His Body, and His Soul left It and went to Limbo.

In the Mass, when the priest consecrates separately the bread and wine, Jesus Christ is not really slain as He was on Calvary, because He can never die any more. His Blood *appears* to be separated from His Body. We call this

"In Memory of Me"

mystical death. You remember what we said about the scapegoat?

It would be a good way of hearing Holy Mass sometimes to think of the sufferings and death of our Lord during it. The priest, when he is saying Mass, continually recalls the Passion of Christ, and our Lord Himself expressed the wish that this should be so.

We could imagine that we were with our Blessed Lady on our way to Calvary, and during Mass we can think of our dear Lord's suffering and death for love of us. Some parts of the Mass remind us very forcibly of the Passion: for instance, when the priest is bowed down at the foot of the altar, we think of Jesus bending beneath the weight of our sins in the Garden of Olives; the kissing of the altar reminds us of the kiss of Judas, and so on through the Mass.

"Behold the Lamb!"

Story.—When Blessed Thomas More was Chancellor of England, in spite of his numerous duties, he always found time each day to hear Mass, and very frequently to serve it. Once during Mass a messenger from the King came to him, saying that His Majesty required to see him at once on a matter of great importance. "Have a little patience," replied Blessed Thomas; "I have not yet completed my homage to a greater King, and I must await the end of the Divine audience."

XII

IN THE SCHOOL OF OUR BLESSED LORD

WHEN some important thing is approaching—Christmas, for example—you do not dream of leaving all your preparations to the last minute. For quite a long time beforehand your mind has been very full of it; you have been making plans, saving money to buy presents, and mother has been ordering all sorts of good things for the great occasion.

Now, our dear Lord was truly Man as well as God, and so we shall not be surprised to find Him doing such wise and good things as we do ourselves. On the

"Behold the Lamb!"

very last night of His life He lets us into a secret. He tells us how full His Sacred Heart has been of the wonderful gift He has all along meant to give us, and which He has reserved to the end. He says: "With desire I have desired to eat this pasch with you before I suffer"; and St. John says beautifully: "Having loved His own who were in the world, He loved them unto the end."

Thinking of these words of our Blessed Lord, we naturally go back over His life to see what signs He has given of this great desire—how He has prepared the people for this gift of the Holy Eucharist. Has He added anything to the teaching which Almighty God had given before the birth into this world of His only Son?

We often use two words about

School of Our Blessed Lord

preparation—*immediate* and *remote*. Preparation for anything is remote when it takes place some time beforehand; for instance, saving your pocket-money is your remote preparation for one side of Christmas. That which is immediate is just before the event takes place—I suppose hanging up your stocking might be an example.

We have remote preparation for the Holy Eucharist all through the ages, and of some kinds we have already spoken. In the next short chapters we are going to speak of that made by our Blessed Lord from the beginning of what is often spoken of as His " public ministry "—that means the last three years of His life, which He spent in. preaching, teaching, and working miracles. We are going to be little pupils in the school of our dear Lord Himself, and learn

"Behold the Lamb!"

from Him some of the wonders contained in the Holy Eucharist.

Story.—The following beautiful legend is about a child Dominican Saint, Blessed Imelda, the patroness of first communicants. When she was a very tiny child she had a great desire to receive our dear Lord in Holy Communion, but was refused on account of her tender years. Time went on, and, though she was clothed in the white wool of St. Dominic, she was not allowed to receive the Lamb of God, of whom her white habit must always have reminded her. One day, as she was crying bitterly because all her companions were approaching the altar, and she alone was denied, suddenly a Sacred Host left the hand of the priest and hovered over the child's head. The priest looked upon

School of Our Blessed Lord

this as a sign of the desire of our Blessed Lord to come into her heart; and, taking the Blessed Sacrament in his hand, he gave It to her.

When the nuns went to rouse her from her thanksgiving, they found the joy had been too great for the loving little heart, and that Jesus had taken her to heaven to make a Communion which never ends.

XIII

A MARRIAGE FEAST

JUST at the very end of the thirty years of Our Lord's hidden life, and when He was beginning His public ministry, He was invited with our Blessed Lady to a wedding, doubtless of some young people whom both knew. Our Lord loves His children to be happy, and so He blessed this feast with His holy Presence.

The bride and bridegroom were so glad to see the brightness and enjoyment of their guests! But after a while there was some uneasiness; the wine was getting very short, and people had not nearly finished. We can imagine how awkward those who knew began to

A Marriage Feast

feel. At last the whisper reached the ears of our Blessed Lady, and, full of sympathy for the discomfort of the family, she went to her Son, and said simply, "They have no wine." She understood Jesus perfectly, and knew that no wish of hers would be unheeded. To the waiters she said, "Whatsoever He shall say to you, do ye."

Our Lord looked round, saw six big water-jars, and told the waiters to fill them with water. Mindful of Mary's words, they immediately filled them to the brim. "Draw out now," said our Blessed Lord, and behold, what they drew was water no longer, but delicious wine! We can imagine their surprise, their admiration and fear, and then their delight at knowing all about where it came from when others were puzzled and asking questions.

"Behold the Lamb!"

They knew that our Lord had changed the substance of water which they had put into the jars into quite another substance, that of wine. He had not created some wine out of nothing, which He might have done, but He changed one thing into another.

The name for this wonderful change of one substance into another is a very long one—it is called Transubstantiation. Only God can make this change.

This was the very first miracle worked by Jesus Christ, and we can easily imagine that at the time He was thinking of another miracle of Transubstantiation to be worked later on. You can see at once what a very striking likeness this bears to the Holy Mass, where our Lord constantly changes one substance into another. At the Consecration in every Mass the substance of bread is

A Marriage Feast

changed into the substance of His Body, and the substance of wine into the substance of His Precious Blood. At this wedding Jesus gave His first lesson on the Holy Mass to His disciples.

Story.—St. Isidore of Madrid was a poor ploughman, who could neither read nor write, but who understood the treasure of Holy Mass, at which he assisted daily. He was once accused of neglecting his work for this purpose, and his master went to the field to find out the truth. There, says the pretty legend, he saw Isidore's plough guided by two angels, ploughing the field while the saint was at Mass.

St. Isidore had a great love for the poor, with whom he constantly shared his food. Once, when all had been given away another poor man appeared.

" Behold the Lamb !"

The saint begged his wife for God's love to try and find the beggar a little soup, and on looking into the vessel she found it had been miraculously refilled.

XIV

BEHIND THE VEILS

DID you wonder why I kept repeating the word *substance* in the last chapter? It was because I wanted to draw your attention to a word which, with another—*accidents*—you will constantly meet with when you read books about the Blessed Sacrament, and I want to make clear to you something of what writers who use these words mean by them.

Let us imagine that you are a boy, and that you have got hold of a large piece of wood. You immediately use your senses to examine it. You find out, perhaps, that it is square, rough, white, with a faint resinous taste and smell.

"Behold the Lamb!"

All these things which you have found out with one or other of your senses are called *accidents*.

Now, suppose that you set about to do something with your piece of wood. You change its shape by carving it into a boat; you plane it until it is smooth to the touch; you change its colour by painting it green; by misadventure you get some turpentine on it, giving it a peculiar taste and smell.

In short, you have quite changed most of the things your senses told you about it. You have changed the accidents, but you know quite well that the wood is still wood.

There was a something over and above those things which you found out, which makes the thing wood, and not something else. This, roughly, is what is meant by *substance*—that some-

Behind the Veils

thing which your senses do not reach, and which makes a thing what it is.

You cannot change substance. You could not change wood into wool.

In the miracle of the marriage feast our Lord changed the substance of the water into the substance of wine. He also changed the accidents of the water—colour, taste, smell—into the accidents of wine. At Holy Mass He changes the substance of the bread into the substance of His Body, but He does not change the accidents of the bread—shape, size, colour, taste, smell—into the accidents of His Body. He changes the substance of the wine into the substance of His Precious Blood, but He does not change the accidents of the wine into the accidents of His Blood.

Was I not right to speak of the *wonders* of Holy Mass?

"Behold the Lamb!"

Our senses of themselves always tell us right about *accidents*. They tell us, for example, that the Sacred Host raised at Mass and given to us in Holy Communion is small, round and white, tasting like wafer-bread, and all that is quite true.

Our senses of sight, hearing, taste, touch, and smell never find out the substance of things, not even of our piece of wood, and so they do not find out the substance of our Lord's Body and Blood in the Holy Eucharist. When speaking of the Blessed Sacrament, instead of the word *accidents*, sometimes other words are used to mean the same thing—for instance, "species," "appearances"; and the Catechism has the phrase "under either *kind*."

Of course, if better words were discovered, the Church would use them.

Behind the Veils

It is not finding two words that seem to explain something which matters, but the thing they stand for; that what appears to be bread and wine is really the true Body and Blood of Jesus Christ, and we believe this because He Himself said so, and the Church teaches it.

Story.—During a cruel persecution of the Christians in China, even the infidels themselves were obliged to acknowledge the wonderful power of the Holy Eucharist. Some of the martyrs were cruelly racked and scourged, their flesh was torn off with red-hot pincers, but they kept repeating the Holy Name of Jesus and professing their faith with undaunted courage. "Truly," said their persecutors, "these men have been eating their enchanted Bread, which casts a spell upon the soul."

XV
IN A DESERT

ONE beautiful day in spring our Blessed Lord took boat and crossed from Capharnaum to the opposite side of the Sea of Galilee. As usual, He was followed by a vast crowd of people all eager to hear Him, to be cured by Him, to tell Him their troubles.

Our Lord talked to them, healed their sick, and comforted the distressed. Everyone was so happy; no one thought of food, or, indeed, of anything connected with this world—the Presence of Jesus took the place of all else. It is almost a shock to find that it is Christ Himself who begins to speak of their need of refreshment.

In a Desert

This is just a little incident which has come down to us, but it is one to remember if ever, when we are in trouble, the devil puts into our heads the thought that God is too great to trouble about our little concerns.

The people are at a distance from a town, and there is no question of buying provisions. The Gospel calls it "the desert," but you must not imagine a small Sahara of desolate sand; it was spring, and there "was much grass" in this place.

At last, St. Andrew announces that he has found a boy who has five loaves and two fishes. That does not seem much good for feeding a crowd of over five thousand persons. However, the little fellow brings what he has to our Lord, who tells the people to sit down on the grass. Then, says St. John, "Jesus

" Behold the Lamb !"

took the loaves, and when He had given thanks, He distributed to them that were set down. In like manner the fishes, as much as they would." Even after that there was enough left to fill twelve baskets.

Would you not love to have been the little boy who gave our Lord the loaves? For one of your favourite feasts you might perhaps ask the priest to be allowed to pay for the altar breads, and offer them to our Blessed Lord to feed the multitude.

This miracle, as well as the one of which we spoke before, was a lesson about the Blessed Sacrament. All over the world are souls asking for the Bread of Life, and all are fed with the Body of Christ; everyone has "as much as he will," and there is always more left. It is never exhausted, no one need ever

In the Desert

go away hungry from our Lord's table.

St. Thomas Aquinas, in a hymn called "Lauda Sion," which forms part of the Mass for the feast of Corpus Christi, says:

> "Be one, or be a thousand fed,
> They eat alike that living Bread,
> Which, still received, ne'er wastes away."

"Jesus took the loaves and gave thanks." How the action must have flashed into the memory of the Apostles at the Last Supper, when once again on that most solemn night Jesus took bread and gave thanks and gave it to them, after having said over it those wondrous words—"This is My Body."

Story.—Many beautiful stories are told of St. Catherine of Siena, a great Dominican Tertiary, and of her loving

"Behold the Lamb!"

hunger for Holy Communion. She lived in the fourteenth century, in days when it was not at all usual to go frequently to Holy Communion. Often when she wished very much to receive our Lord, she would say to Blessed Raymund of Capua, who was her confessor, "Father, I am hungry; for the love of God feed my soul." She once told another priest, "When I cannot receive Holy Communion, I go into the church and watch before the Blessed Sacrament, and sometimes I am refreshed by the mere presence of a priest who has touched the Sacred Host."

XVI

A PROMISE

Not even the smallest of you but knows perfectly well what a promise is. How secure we feel of being favourably heard when we are begging for some pleasure, if we can plead that " it was a promise !" How satisfied we immediately are if one whom we trust promises us something!

Now, before the time came for really giving the Blessed Sacrament, our dear Lord *promised* it, and that is what we are going to speak about next. First, however, I want to ask you whether it has ever happened to you to have a secret which you were keeping, and

" Behold the Lamb !"

which you thought would give great pleasure to some people you loved? You were full of it for a long time before, but at last the day you had been so looking forward to came, and, radiant with happiness, you told your cherished secret.

Then . . . no one was a bit pleased, some were angry with you, and there was a good deal of bother. How did you feel? It was as if all the joy had been suddenly wiped from your face and heart; the tears were near; when you were alone, perhaps in bed, they flowed freely, and they were very bitter, you were so disappointed.

You know that our Lord was truly man; His Sacred Heart was a human heart, and could be hurt and suffer like our own. At the Last Supper He told His Apostles how full His Heart had

A Promise

always been of the great Gift He was then giving them. But He did not wait until then to speak of it; the very day after He had fed the people in the desert with the miraculous bread, when they sought Him again, He spoke to them of the Bread of Life, and promised to give them His Body and Blood as food for their souls, though He did not at that time tell them *how*.

This wonderful talk is given us by St. John in the sixth chapter of his Gospel. I will tell you one or two verses, and you must look for the rest. Jesus said to the Jews:

"The Bread of God is that which cometh down from heaven, and giveth life to the world. ... I am the Bread of Life. ... I am the Living Bread which came down from heaven. ... The Bread that I will give is My flesh

"Behold the Lamb!"

for the life of the world. . . . He that eateth My flesh and drinketh My blood hath everlasting life, and I will raise him up in the last day."

Now, do you think all the people were delighted; that over and over again they thanked our dear Lord for so wonderful a Gift? No! it is all horrible. They began to argue, to dispute amongst themselves as to whether He *could* do it; they said it was too hard for them to believe; a lot of them left Him, and, St. John says, "walked no more with Him."

Jesus even turned to the twelve Apostles and asked them if they were going away too, but St. Peter answered for them all that they believed in Him, in what He was and what He said. These are St. Peter's words: "Lord, to whom shall we go? Thou hast the

A Promise

words of eternal life. And we have believed and have known that Thou art the Christ, the Son of God."

Story.—Once, when a number of clever men had a great dispute about the Blessed Sacrament, they decided to ask St. Thomas Aquinas, the great Dominican doctor, to settle it. He had all the different opinions put into writing, so that he might understand the other side. Then, after much prayer and penance, he wrote an answer. When it was finished, he took what he had written into the church, laid it before the tabernacle, and asked our Blessed Lord to make known to him whether what he had said was true, and not to allow him to teach any error. Some other Dominicans who were present tell us that Jesus answered his prayer by saying: "Thou

"Behold the Lamb!"

hast written worthily of the Sacrament of My Body."

Another time, also, our Lord told him he had written well, and asked him what reward he would like. St. Thomas gave this beautiful answer: "None other than Thyself, O Lord."

XVII

A MAN WITH A PITCHER

HAVE any of you had a brother made a priest since you can remember? Perhaps he came to say his first Mass in the church at home, and you helped with the preparations.

I knew a young priest who had a mother and several sisters, and for such a long time before he was ordained they were working hard, preparing. He came home to say his first Mass, and every bit of linen for the altar, the tabernacle curtains, and veil for the ciborium, as well as the alb and amice he wore, had all been made by the clever, loving fingers of those at home while he had been away studying.

"Behold the Lamb!"

Well, the time had come for our dear Lord to say the first Mass which had ever been said in the world, and St. Luke tells us some very interesting things about the preparations. I think you will like his own words: "And the day of the unleavened bread came, on which it was necessary that the pasch (the little lamb) should be killed. And He sent Peter and John, saying: Go and prepare for us the pasch, that we may eat.

"But they said: Where wilt Thou that we prepare?

"And He said to them: Behold, as you go into the city, there shall meet you a man carrying a pitcher of water; follow him into the house where he entereth in. And you shall say to the goodman of the house: The Master saith to thee, Where is the guest-

A Man with a Pitcher

chamber, where I may eat the pasch with My disciples? And he will show you a large dining-room, furnished; and there prepare.

"And they going, found as He had said to them, and made ready the pasch."

Do you notice that Jesus, Who was so poor that He had "not where to lay His head," chose a large room, furnished, for His first Mass? And did you also notice which two Apostles Jesus chose —Peter and John? St. Peter was the Apostle of Faith; he it was who so boldly confessed our Lord to be the Son of God. Once Jesus asked them, "Whom do men say that I am?" And after they had answered that question, He said: "And whom do you say that I am?" St. Peter replied, "Thou art the Christ, the Son of the living God." Again, after the "Promise," Jesus asked,

"Behold the Lamb!"

"Will you also go away?" And St. Peter made his profession of faith once more, and in almost the same words.

St. John is the Apostle of Purity and Love. It was to him that Jesus, dying, confided His stainless Virgin Mother. Our Lord Himself had said, "Blessed are the clean of heart, for they shall see God." And it was St. John who recognized Jesus first when, after His resurrection, He gave the wonderful catch of fishes. St. John said to the others, "It is the Lord."

He was "the disciple whom Jesus loved" best, and who, on account of his love and purity, was allowed at the Last Supper to rest his head on the Sacred Heart.

Do you not see what a wonderful fitness there was in St. Peter and St. John's preparing for the first Mass, since the

A Man with a Pitcher

virtues of faith and purity and love are the virtues we need most when we approach the Blessed Sacrament; they are connected in such a marvellous way that I once heard it said, "Faith is the purity of the mind, just as purity is the faith of the body."

Story.—Of all the saints, perhaps the one most intimately connected in our mind with the Blessed Sacrament is St. Thomas Aquinas, the dear saint who wrote the beautiful Office of Corpus Christi, and the hymn "Adoro Te." He, like St. John, was remarkable for his spotless purity. A very pretty story is connected with this. Once, while he was praying that he might never sin against this holy virtue, two angels came and bound a white cord tightly round his waist, at the same time telling

" Behold the Lamb !"

him that God had heard his prayer, and would preserve him even from temptation. He knew that purity is a gift straight from the hands of God, and he wore the cord all his life, because he knew that pain is the best thing to keep that lily white.

XVIII

THE WORK OF A SLAVE

In the country in which our dear Lord lived the people did not have shoes and stockings like yours, but, instead, wore sandals. Now, often for a long time together there was no rain there, nor were there plenty of water-carts, such as we have in the dry weather at home. So you will understand that the roads were often very dusty, and that in walking along a good deal of dust would get into the sandals, making the feet hot, soiled, and uncomfortable. Does not that happen to you with the sand, when you are at the seaside?

In Palestine, if anyone came to the

"Behold the Lamb!"

house, the first thing done for him was to take off his sandals and pour cooling water over his feet; this was the duty, not of an important person, but of one of the inferior slaves. You can understand now why, when St. John the Baptist wanted to make people realize how great Jesus Christ was, he said that he, whom all the people thought a great prophet, was not worthy even to take off our Lord's sandals.

Now, let us go back to the "large dining-room, furnished," to which Jesus had come towards evening. At this Last Supper He is going to give His Apostles their first Communion, and make them priests. Would you not like to know what was the "immediate preparation" He made with them?

It is St. John who tells us. Often when he is going to relate some saying

The Work of a Slave

or event, he begins with something which seems to have nothing to do with it, and then, when we have thought a little, we see it has everything to do with it.

St. John begins by telling us that Jesus knew how powerful He was, and that He was the Son of God, and then immediately he says that this great and holy Lord put off His long outer garment, took a basin of water and a towel, and, kneeling down, began to wash the feet of His Apostles. A beautiful tradition tells us that when He had dried them He bent His head and pressed His Divine lips to those feet in a kiss.

He came and knelt before St. Peter, but the Apostle of Faith could not bear it; he tried to prevent it, and it was only when Jesus threatened that he should "have no part" with Him that

"Behold the Lamb!"

St. Peter gave in, and wanted to be washed even more.

Our Lord Himself told them some of His reasons for doing this. First, that they might be "wholly clean," teaching us with what purity of soul we should approach the altar.

Then He reminded them that He who had washed their feet was their Lord and Master. He had even earlier told them to learn of Him to be "humble of heart."

And, lastly, He says it was for an example, that they should do for others what He had done for them. Even in this country we can sometimes do for others exactly what our Lord did for His Apostles. It happens occasionally that persons who have to be got ready for the Last Sacraments need to have their feet washed for them. If we are

The Work of a Slave

ever privileged to render this service to anyone, we should try to do it as our dear Lord did.

And once every year, on Maundy Thursday, every Bishop, every Catholic King and Queen, and the head of nearly every religious community, washes the feet of others in memory of Jesus Christ.

Story.—In your history-books, have you read about the great Saint Thomas of Canterbury, whom you perhaps know better as Thomas à Becket? When he was made Archbishop of Canterbury, he felt that it was not a good thing to live any longer in the splendid style which had been becoming to the Lord Chancellor of England.

He laid aside his rich garments and put on a monk's habit, under which he

"Behold the Lamb!"

wore a rough hair shirt. He ate coarse food, and every day entertained at his table twelve poor beggars, whose feet he washed in honour of the humility of Jesus Christ.

THE MYSTERY OF FAITH.

To face p. 101.

XIX
CORPUS CHRISTI

We are going to talk about the first Mass, the wonderful rite which was to give to the world the Body of Christ, His Real Presence in the world to-day, and all the days that are since gone, or are yet to come.

It is such a great, such a wonderful, but, above all, such a loving thing that it seems as if we hardly ought to talk about it, but just take God's Holy Book, and, kneeling before the altar, read about it secretly, with no one but Jesus Himself near to watch us, because we should be shy for anyone else to see all we feel about the Blessed Sacrament.

"Behold the Lamb!"

In your New Testament you would find all about that Last Supper told over and over again—four times. Jesus in the Blessed Sacrament was to be everything to our souls, and so He has seen to it that we shall be told with greatest care what He did for us on that night.

We are told how they ate the little lamb which had been sacrificed, and which was a type of the Sacrifice of the Cross, to take place on the morrow. We are told how sad our dear Lord was; there is something peculiarly terrifying in the sadness of Him who is the source of all our joy. When He is sad, to whom can we turn for happiness?

I will take just the Gospel account of what happened next. St. Luke says: "And taking bread, He gave thanks, and broke, and gave to them, saying, THIS IS MY BODY, which is given for

Corpus Christi

you. Do this for a commemoration of Me. In like manner the chalice also, after He had supped, saying, This is the chalice, the new testament in My Blood, which shall be shed for you."

With those simple words, "This is My Body," He, who by a word had wrought creation, gave to us His most wonderful gift of Himself, and when He said, "Do this in commemoration of Me," He made His first priests, who would see that the Body of Christ never failed us.

You know that *Corpus Christi* is the Latin for *Body of Christ*, do you not? The holy Curé of Ars, when he saw the spire of a church, used to say, "God is there, because the priest has passed by."

No one but our dear Lord Himself can really make you understand all that the Blessed Sacrament is, and that is why I beg you again and again, dear little

"Behold the Lamb!"

reader, whoever you may be, to read and think about Jesus in the Tabernacle there at His feet, for no school is like the school of our Blessed Lord, and none are so well taught as they who are "taught of God."

Story.—After our Lord had given His Apostles their first Communion He had a long and loving talk with them, during which He said, "I will not now call you servants ... but I have called you friends," and we will end this part of our little talks together in the company of St. Dominic, who loved our dear Lord so tenderly and chivalrously that he has been given the glorious title of the "Friend of Jesus Christ." In his life we can find beautiful examples of those virtues of which we have just been speaking.

Corpus Christi

His *Faith* was so great that he founded an Order for the express purpose of spreading the Truth about our Blessed Lord, and he gave his followers the word *Truth* for their motto.

When he died he had never lost his baptismal innocence; his *Purity* was like that of a white lily, and so in one of his hymns we sing, "Stainless as a virgin lily."

His *Love* for Jesus in the Holy Eucharist was so great that all the time he could snatch from his many duties was spent with his Friend. He had no cell of his own, but when everyone else had left the church and gone to bed, he remained on, and when at last he took his short sleep, it was stretched on the altar steps, still near to Jesus in the Blessed Sacrament.

www.ingramcontent.com/pod-product-compliance
Lightning Source LLC
Chambersburg PA
CBHW020012050426
42450CB00005B/427